Our Shades Of Black History

Individual Stories From Black Men & Women From Moments In Time

Our Shades Of Black History
Stories From Black Men & Women From Moments In Time
Volume II

by Crystal Dionne Williams,
Jarvis T. Booker,
Nichol Mills,
& Tamula Blue

JumpTime Publishing LLC
Publishers since 2021
Houston, TX

jtp@jumptimepublishing.com

Copyright © 2024 by Crystal Dionne Williams, Jarvis T. Booker, Nichol Mills, Tamula Blue

Title: Our Shades Of Black History: Stories From Moments In Time (Volume II)

Edited By:
JumpTime Publishing & Renee Wells

All Right Reserved

ISBN: 979-8-9910857-0-0

Our books may be purchased in bulk for promotional, educational, or business use. Please contact your local book seller or JumpTime Publishing by email at jtp@jumptimepublishing.com.

No part of this book may be reproduced, or stored in a retrieval system, or transmitted in any form or by any means, electronic, mechanical, photocopying, recording, or otherwise, without the expressed written permission of the publisher and author.

This book is dedicated to those who have experienced life's good and bad, but still persevered!

Table Of Contents

Introduction

1. Moments In Time That Will Never Be Forgotten - By Crystal Dionne Williams

2. Infinite Potential - By Jarvis T. Booker

3. My Superpower: Childhood Trauma Is My Superpower By Nichol Mills

4. When I Got The News - By Tamula Blue

Author Pages

Black History
Is
American History!

Introduction

Every story is essential—*Our Shades of Black History Vol. II* is a brick in the creation of timeless pieces of history. With every day we move forward, it has become increasingly important that history is recorded. Just as important as the recordation of history is that history is recorded accurately.

Publishing stories by authors from diverse backgrounds is essential to demonstrating our contribution to society and the meaningful messages that each author wanted to leave for the world.

Our Shades of Black History are stories from Black men and women who felt it necessary to leave the world with a part of their story from just a moment in time. Each story speaks to the lived experiences and triumphs of each author. This book is Volume II of the original book, Our Shades of Black History.

Our Shades of Black History is American history, stories written by those who happen to be Black. No story shall be left behind!

Our Shades of Black History!

Our Shades Of Black History
Stories From Black Men & Women From Moments In Time
Volume II

by Crystal Dionne Williams,
Jarvis T. Booker,
Nichol Mills,
& Tamula Blue

Moments In Time That Will Never Be Forgotten

By Crystal Dionne Williams

There are days in our lives that we will always be able to remember. Well, April 9, 2023, was a day that I will never forget. It was the day that changed my life forever. It was a day that I had been trying to prepare myself for emotionally for nearly two years. I was not anticipating it, but I knew it was inevitable, and I did not know when the time would come. How can you prepare for the death of someone who you've known all your life? The person who gave you life? Looking back, each visit leading up to this day was crucial and necessary. At the time, everything seemed or appeared to be a blur, but months later, I remember even the smallest detail.

A little backstory. My mother raised my sister and me in New Jersey. Once we became young adults and moved away, my mother eventually retired and moved back to her hometown. She grew up in a small city in South Georgia. The timing of her moving was perfect. Our grandmother was aging and needed someone to be with her regularly. After my mom retired, it seemed logical that moving to Georgia was a good idea. However, for my sister and I, traveling to her was more complex because no major airport for miles existed. Each time I visited, it would involve a whole day trip in a car or a flight and a three to four hour ride from the closest major airport.

My mother always had her arms open to help family and friends when she could and at times when she couldn't and shouldn't have. It was the type of person that she was. As long as I can remember she was always lending a helping hand and going above and beyond to make others feel special. My mother listened when people spoke. She would also be so thoughtful in saying and doing the right thing for others at the opportune times. I would like to say that her great cooking always warmed the hearts of many. She always made big servings of food and put a smile on the face of family and friends when they devoured her meals. People remember her as just being a kind person with a sweet heart.

She also worked just as hard as she helped others. My mother worked for years at Newark Airport. Sometimes, she worked around the clock. As a single parent, she wanted to make sure that my sister and I had everything we needed and then some. My mother was stern and definitely imprinted the idea that hard work can pay off. She ensured that my sister and I performed well in school and kept to our household chores. She showed us that our hard work did not go unnoticed. My mother gave us a weekly allowance for our efforts. She also taught us about responsibility as she would provide us with our lunch and snack money daily, and it was up to us not to lose it. Some would say we had it made as kids. By the time I reached age 14, we had traveled to Jamaica, the Bahamas on the Big Red Boat, and Hawaii. However, that did not stop us from experiencing heartache and some of the woes that other families experienced throughout life.

I recall when my oldest sister became very ill. My younger sister and I were in high school. My mother would get up every morning during the week to make sure we were off to school, go to work, and then drive over an hour to a New York hospital to be with my very sick sister. This was the routine for months until my sister was released from the hospital. My mother would spend much of her time shuffling back and forth to make sure my eldest sister was taken care of until the very day of our sister's passing. We hardly saw her, but she ensured we had what we needed in her absence. She sacrificed a lot during that time, as she always did.

In 2019, my immediate family experienced a tremendous change that left me devastated. My mother flew to New Jersey within a couple of days to be with me and my children, and she did not leave our side until she was certain that we were okay. She selflessly spent months attending to our every need. This just was the type of person that she was. She showed up when you needed her the most. She put everything to the side to be there.

No one was prepared for the COVID-19 global emergency that turned into a pandemic. It changed our life and the lives of many forever. Living in New Jersey, I saw first-hand the early devastation of the pandemic. While New York was the focal point, as it was a hot spot, I would learn through social media that many of my childhood friends lost loved ones during the early stages of the pandemic. It was a rough time because things were shutting down, and traveling was not easy at the time or throughout the pandemic.

In the late summer of 2020, my mother became ill with COVID-19. She had been placed on a ventilator, and we, as a family, were a nervous wreck. Later, my mother would go on to develop heart concerns. She would end up having multiple surgeries to remove blood clots and had a defibrillator placed in her heart. She spent a lot of time in rehabilitation in the months afterward, and things seemed to be going in the right direction.

After my mother was released from the rehabilitation center, she received assistance and support that was funded by her insurance and other programs. However, as part of the American health system, when her insurance stopped paying for all of the assistance, that meant all of the rehabilitation and therapy stopped. My mother was abruptly cut off from most of her much-needed care. She was left with very little assistance.

Our cousin spent a lot of time helping my mother in our absence. She informed us that the program helping my mother said she was okay alone. However, only two weeks after all of the assistance was removed, she ended up back in the hospital.

Once my mother returned to the rehabilitation center--which at times seemed to contribute to my mother's repeated hospital stays—we were told that she was becoming very ill. While in the rehabilitation center, we had to figure out what the next step was going to be. My mother's insurance would only cover her rehabilitation stay for so long. However, we knew that she could not live by herself any longer.

After what we now realized was another unnecessary trip to the hospital, we ultimately decided that my mother's ailments had gotten to the point where she needed 24-hour care. That meant we had two options-Hospice or a nursing home. Not liking the idea of Hospice and my mother wholly not agreeing with it, we opted for the nursing home.

Today, we realize that nursing homes are understaffed and lack some of the resources needed to properly care for our elderly when they are most in need. Once my mother was placed in the nursing home, she was in and out of the hospital many times. It was a daily up and down struggle just to keep her stable and, in our opinion, alive. Not being there every day to see my mother, her condition, and the treatment from the care facility was hard. We often had to rely on family and friends nearby to check on our mother when it was difficult to reach anyone at the nursing home facility, which happened very often.

When your loved one gets as sick as my mother was, sometimes you have to make hard decisions. Sometimes, you have to choose and go on routes you can't imagine. One thing my sister and I had to deal with, and we decided to deal with early on, was planning my mother's funeral. We knew that she had less time here and did not know what we would expect or the emotions that we would be feeling when she passed. My sister and I made a conscious choice to plan her funeral before she passed. It's hard to imagine picking out your mother's casket when she is still here, breathing and talking. But it is something that had to be done or at least something we thought was the best thing to do at the time.

Also, during this time, my sister and I both went to Georgia to be with my mother for what would end up being her last five months here. My sister handled most of the written paperwork. I was the one who went to the funeral home and made most of the arrangements. I did it by myself, and it was really hard on me. But we were able to get through it together.

My sister and I worked together and brought our children to Georgia. We rotated working remotely and tending to our mother and children while we were there. We devised a plan for the upcoming months and how we would alternate months, checking on our mother. We prepared to leave on the same day, Saturday, April 8, one day before Easter. My mother had been sent back to the hospital the day before (due to what we now believe was neglect), but we decided that it would be okay to leave since my sister was planning to return the following weekend. We thought that she would have round-the-clock care since she was in the hospital. She also had her family and friends there in Georgia, to whom we are so grateful, who would look after her in our absence.

On the morning of April 9, 2023, things seemed pretty normal. I spoke with my sister earlier that morning. It was Easter

Sunday, and I was back home in New Jersey. Nothing could have prepared me for the phone call I received that afternoon. The doctor called and told me that my mother was no longer here. It was the most challenging piece of news that one could ever get. My heart was shattered, and I had to tell my sister, who I knew would be equally shattered.

It's hard to explain what it feels like to lose someone close to you. It's even harder to explain when you lose your mother. Particularly when you are as close to your mother as I was, it's like all you can think about is, I can't believe they're not here. You play all of the special moments back to yourself. The days and weeks after that seem to happen really fast. My mother looked beautiful at her funeral, and I knew that she would be happy with how my sister, and I sent her off. She is and will be greatly missed.

The one thing I realize is that sometimes you can become numb to the pain that you might feel, and then poof, it hits you like an oncoming train. Over the last year, I have learned that I'll always miss my mother. She is the only person that I know inside out, literally. The great person that she was to me, my sisters, and all the people who knew her will always be remembered.

Jani Jani gone, but never forgotten!

Infinite Potential

By Jarvis T. Booker
CEO of BOOKER HTX REAL ESTATE INSPECTIONS, PLLC

Since the earliest days that I can remember, I've loved challenging the usual ways of thinking about success. I've always believed you can expand your knowledge and understanding by exploring the world from different angles and perspectives. True happiness isn't just about reaching a goal. It's also about how we live every day, building bridges to the things that we genuinely love.

Here, within these pages, I want you to feel my story, not just read it—the relentless struggle against adversity, the weight of prejudice, and the suffocating grip of stereotypes. There was a time when I believed that every painful moment in life was just another link added to the heavy chain that was constantly pulling me down. Ironically, they turned out to be the very catalyst that forged my evolution and tattooed the spirit of infinite potential on my heart and into my soul.

These discouraging moments in my life birthed a phoenix that continues to rise through the flames and ashes as its wings grow bigger and stronger each time this world attempts to bind it with fiery chains. These trials unearthed not just success and joy but, above all else, an enduring understanding that every hardship, every setback. My trials become a battleground, shaping my ascent and revealing the resilience and infinite potential born within.

"Understanding" is encapsulated with patience and faith, which is the art of knowing rather than hoping. You must have a faith that cannot be shaken or doubtful, a "knowing" faith, not a "hoping" faith. Your belief in a higher power that is part of your soul and your spirit and dwells within your being is an immense power to yield during the unavoidably uncomfortable phases of elevation.

    My wife tells me that I was a manmaid in my past life, which is a man mermaid. I love the beach, I love the ocean, I love swimming, especially without the restriction of a life jacket. As soon as I get the opportunity, I walk to the beach and embrace the scent of the ocean in the air. As I get closer, I feel the warm sand between my toes. Then, I get closer to the shoreline, and the sand turns cold. That first wave that hits my ankles is so cold that I run back for a second, laughing and saying, "It's Freezing." Finally, I gather myself accordingly and say, "Forget It." I run further into the beach, high-stepping erratically and off balance. Then I take a deep breath, hold it, and launch myself over a wave and into another world underwater. I put my hands together in front of me, imagine I have fins, close my fingers, then pull back with force as my body thrust forward effortlessly through the ocean as if I were meant to be here. As I am gliding and slicing through this remarkable world, I see schools of fish, crabs, shells, and flounder bubbles rising from under the sand. I feel a type of euphoric freedom and peace when I'm in the water.

    I would never experience this if I took my dad's advice. When he knows I'm going on vacation, he gives me a spill about the dangers of the ocean. "Be careful, son, don't swim too far out; that undercurrent is strong and could pull you into the ocean." "Be careful, son, watch for jellyfish; they are hard to see, so think twice about getting in that water." "Be careful, son; I was reading about flesh-eating bacteria on those beaches." My dad doesn't know how to swim and is terrified of the water. His advice is based on his upbringing, past environments, and experiences, but most prevalent is that it's based on his fears and insecurities.

Advice comes from people's personal baggage rather than giving the unbiased information and knowledge about the situation. That type of advice discourages me because I'm such an optimistic being, and I thrive on taking the path least traveled rather than playing it safe. I am more receptive to advice modeled around the possibility of overcoming obstacles and not being consumed by them.

Comfort and elevation never walk hand in hand – I urge you to recall a moment when you soared to new heights without discomfort. I reiterate: 'There is no way to comfortably ascend to new heights,' hence acknowledging the necessity to embrace discomfort as an integral part of progress. Understanding that there is no comfortable way to cultivate the strength, mindset, and passion necessary to sustain or maintain and actively nurture and thrive within the legacy one aims to build. Recognizing that the journey toward uncovering invaluable insights, intangible gems, and enlightenment will be contingent entirely upon persevering through trials, tribulations, mistakes, discouragement, frustration, and societal norms. Embracing being uncomfortable during these times not only profoundly shapes our careers, happiness, and financial aspirations but also defines the core of our very existence.

I have always questioned societal constructs, cliche perspectives of success, and most of all…the generalized interpretations of this personal journey that we all must travel on and through individually called…. life. Merriam-Webster defines advice as a "recommendation regarding a decision or course of conduct." I have mixed feelings about that definition because advice in specific contexts and aspects of life is subjective and not always objective. When it comes to people asking for advice regarding aspects of their life or a life-altering decision, I tend to tell them I can't give them advice, but I can provide them with information they can decipher and apply accordingly.

    I grew up in a small country town that's really easy to get trapped in if you don't develop a plan and a way out. Elevation, wealth, and success were never the main focal points or topics of discussion in the sense of legally creating financial stability and generational wealth. Most of the teachings and advice I was given were more or less about going to college, obtaining a certification in a trade, or setting yourself up to work for a prominent refinery. That was the advice given regarding the legal paths to have a great career. However, I also got advice about how to accomplish financial advancement quickly and easily through some very creative illegal activities. Though my hometown was known for farming, trail rides, rodeos, and the old black cowboy circuits, we were also known for a common epidemic that is known in most places of poverty and a shortage of resources. That epidemic is crack cocaine. As bad as that sounds, it's unlike what you see in movies such as New Jack City, Paid in Full, and Menace to Society.

    These aren't strangers that you pass by and shake your head in shame; these are the people that you grew up knowing and loving, your family and your friends. It was normalized, and when something is normalized, you don't see it as a vice. You see it as just another part of life that just so happens to spin out of control and ruin a life, but it has also been known to yield monetary gain. In every town, in every city across the world, there will be drugs bought and drugs sold. It devastates communities, but it is also seen as a financial opportunity for those who normalized this and adapted to their environment.

Let me explain: if you grew up in a town where obesity was an issue and every family that you knew had a few obese people. You've seen these people since you were a toddler; from a young age, you see these same individuals eating burgers, milkshakes, and fries. You turn twelve years old, and you witness teenagers that you look up to getting paid to pick up their food and deliver it. You're not looking at it as ruining your community, promoting unhealthy living, and assisting your friends and family in their journey to diabetes or obesity when you decide to capitalize off of their vice. You justify it as an opportunity to offer a service that supplies the local demands that are always in demand. You've seen these people buy unhealthy food regardless, so you decide to get a slice of the pie they're already eating.

I grew up with two family members that were addicted to drugs. I love them both to death and have nothing wrong to say about them, but one of my uncles was a high-functioning addict who hid his addiction very well, and I never knew until I got older. He worked a corporate job, has a family, and is looked at with the utmost respect by me and my cousins, yet he's a smoker. The other, well, the other, is just more transparent about his vice. He didn't try to hide it, but he also went to certain extremes that were close to the edge of the cliff of morality whenever he was having a bad day, but he has a heart of gold.

Amidst all this, there was a smoker named Chucky Reynolds. I don't know if that was his real name, but we called him that. He was a neighborhood smoker with a knack for various trades, from fixing cars to mowing lawns and construction. He knew a little bit about everything despite battling addiction. Once, I asked him to cut some weeds out of my grandmother's ditch, and he said, "If a man can do it, I can do it... 'cause I'm a man." I said, "C'mon, Chucky, with the riddles and answer the question so I can tell my grandma if you're going to do it." He said, "I did answer you. Now, if there somebody out there that can do it, a man out in this world can get rid of those weeds?" I said, "Yes! Chucky! I'm sure there's a man out in this world that can do that." He says, "Well, if a man can do it, then I can do it 'cause you're looking at a man! And God made me in his image, so I'm pretty sure he will bless me with all I need to cut them weeds out the ditch for ya grandma!" Chucky had it done in a couple of hours.

Those words stuck with me my whole life, reminding me that with the right mindset, anything is achievable. So, if you noticed, he gave me information and inspiration, not advice. It was well received. Ironically, Chucky Reynolds, who had an addiction.... with all his struggles, became my source of motivation. His diverse skills and words inspired me to set ambitious goals, transcending the challenges of my environment, especially since I witnessed him do so much with so little in the same environment.

Against the odds, I graduated high school at 16 and joined the Army. I enlisted as a 31C communications engineer for signal corps and field artillery. I was sent to basic training in Fort Sill, Lawton, OK. I kept the bar high because if it was just out of my reach, it constantly pushed me to strive for something beyond my past. The first thing I remember experiencing in the Army was the actual ride to basic training called "The Cattle Run." The name cattle run is very fitting for the experience that was felt by all the privates, aka "Fresh Meat." They would put about 12 of us in this cattle trailer with metal slats on the sides that obscure your vision only to see a small glimpse of daylight and snippets of unrecognizable buildings.

As they drove us to our living quarters, which are called barracks, they randomly made left and right turns as if we were hostages, and they didn't want us to remember the route to the hideout. As soon as they stopped the vehicles, the doors popped open, and about six drill sergeants were yelling and spitting orders at you while you scurried out toe to heel like cattle. This moment was meant to be filled with high intensity and anxiety to test if you can take orders while in a high-pressure situation. It's also a bit of traditional hazing as well because some of the faces and reactions of my battle buddies were hilarious.

I remained cool, calm, and collected and just numbed my ears to the yelling. Instead, I listened to the instructions rather than paying attention to the spit flying and veins popping out of their necks and foreheads. They wanted to show us how to remain calm and follow orders under stress, but most of all, they could weed out the ones who initially buckled during this test to monitor them and strengthen their weaknesses during training. They also identified some of us who had leadership skills by seeing if we would help others in need if we finished the task early. In hindsight, I believe it was very strategic and conducive to grooming us to stay calm, think clearly, and execute tasks in stressful, intense situations. That experience allowed me to survive and overcome many circumstances throughout my life.

I've learned so many things while serving in the US Army that impacted the trajectory of my life in the most subtle and obvious ways. Here is a quote from my leadership in the Army that I've lived by and I can't seem to forget, even if I tried:

"The 5 Ps of life:
Prior Planning Prevents Poor Performance- Plans are organized thoughts that are projected into the future by foreseeing cause and affects, that lead to a calculated probability of success or execution. Without proper planning you increase the probability of failure. Set yourself up for success, organize your thoughts into plans."

I could break down each piece of the quote and apply it to life for you, but I found that it hits home and sticks when you get your own personal perspective and understanding.

    I enlisted in the Army at a very young age. I didn't have the same life experiences as others in high school at the latter part of their maturity into adulthood. I was still a kid, so my experiences in the military definitely molded me into who I would be as an adult. I went in with the bravado of someone who was confident in his mindstate being unbreakable. Before I knew it, I was screaming at the top of my lungs with the same spit flying and veins popping that I saw in the soldiers the first day of training. I have been converted. I am no longer a seventeen-year-old boy trying to go through the motions with this military "huah blah blah" for the GI Bill to pay for college. I've become something else now. I am a warrior, indestructible, mentally and emotionally unbreakable, a sharpened WEAPON.

    I've come to realize something profound: while rules are important, the misuse of authority is a whole different story. Whether in the military, corporate America, or blue-collar jobs, I've witnessed bosses, supervisors, and managers abusing their power. It's like they forget we're all adults, deserving of respect. When someone talks down to you, you know that feeling, questioning your intelligence and dignity? It's infuriating. But I refuse to accept it. We're meant to stand tall, demanding the same respect we bestow onto others. I refuse to bow to the meekness instilled in Black Americans since the inception of slavery.

Education is one cutting tool that may not cut the entire shackle off our ankles, but it can weaken the chain. I attended Prairie View A&M University with the desire to obtain a degree in biomedical engineering. I envisioned creating prosthetic organs, such as hearts, kidneys, and livers, that could sustain and function in the human body. While in college, I was also a soldier in the Army National Guard. I was set to deploy to Iraq during my sophomore year. This halted my vision of becoming a biomedical engineer. I wasn't too far from my love for figuring out how systems are built and work together because the military trained me in communications engineering. I don't think I would have been as hungry as I am for learning and elevation without that taste of education, college life, independence, and responsibility.

Having an education can open doors for you and give you opportunities to obtain a great career, positions, and roles that will allow you to build your leadership skills. The skills that you learn in leadership roles are transferable to endeavors outside of working for an employer. If you analyze the strengths and weaknesses of the industry that you are in, you can then create a better model that can ultimately yield a better quality of life for you and your family. Tapping into the benefits of being an entrepreneur allows you to take advantage of utilizing your skills to make a living working for yourself rather than letting your skills and abilities be used for another person's benefit.

I've always felt like my purpose on earth was to bless others and hopefully change or at least "bump" the trajectory of the next generation in a positive direction. I've always believed the most direct way for me to do that is with my children first. Truth be told, it was my children who impacted the trajectory of my life and have been one of the biggest blessings of my life. I have a total of six children. My first four are from my previous marriage: Three daughters aged twenty-one, seventeen, and sixteen years old, and one son who is fifteen years old. My wife and I also have two children: a bonus son and a newborn.

It bothers me when I hear parents say, "If I didn't have kids, I would have... blah blah blah." I have developed and matured enough to see opportunities that one may not have had at a certain point in your life. All of my children are a part of my personal development. My kids have shifted my mindstate to another level. My children have given me a sense of responsibility for another person I may not have had when I didn't have children.

As I made different transitions in life, becoming a better person and father for my children was at the forefront of my decision-making. The decision to focus on going back to school to get a degree and create a better life for them was important. I received my manufacturing engineering and process technology degree and numerous certifications. I grinded in college and was awarded the presidential honors award for manufacturing engineering, which caught the attention of Chevron Phillips. I was offered an internship and got a job with the company.

My career was sought after by many people, so I felt blessed and honored to have that opportunity. However, I also knew that I would not be there for the long haul. It just wasn't in me to work for another person's dream for that long, so I had a seven-year plan. However, after five years, the environment, people, politics, perceptions, and lack of quality of life took its toll. The job became so overwhelming that I needed therapy for the amount of anxiety and stress that I developed during the last year of my employment there.

At some point, it was apparent that my spirit was not content with the atmosphere and degradation of character that was being projected toward me almost daily. I'm sure everyone has had that one day when you get tired of bearing that weight of the mask you've been wearing. That mask gets heavy, you know, the mask that I'm talking about. The one that you put on every day you go to work, that hides your true self, your personality, your spirit, your sense of humor, your sensitivity, even your love. Love is the hardest thing to hide daily because love and kindness are considered weaknesses when attempting to ascend the corporate ladder. I yearned to be able to be myself, whereas I worked so hard for years to break through personal issues. I just wanted to instill kindness and positivity, be supportive of peers, and be lighthearted and genuine daily without hiding my true self. However, I operated in an industry that appeared to attack at the slightest sign of weakness.

The culture was so negative and judgmental that you literally had to have the mindstate of protecting yourself at all times…. all the time. Protect yourself from ridicule, embarrassment, tempers, conflicts, drama, politics, perceptions, racism, elite circles, degradation, disrespect, belittlement, and being the butt-end of the joke of the day. Maybe I didn't have tough skin, perhaps I was sensitive, maybe I couldn't take the daily barrage of jokes with the undertone of insult. Or perhaps I personally can't flourish in an environment where I have to numb myself from feeling like a King to normalizing feeling inferior. I had enough stress outside of work and didn't have the capacity to add more stress to my plate from work, and it started to affect me negatively.

I realized that I wasn't taking care of myself, my wife, my kids, or my family. No matter how much I've accomplished, as a man in the present day, I felt I was not taking care of myself nor my family. Chevron Phillips, my job, was the head of my family. Therefore, Chevron Phillips was taking care of my family. I felt that my kids couldn't depend on me if my success were dependent upon a job that was costing me my mental health. It rang so loud over and over in my head. "MY FAMILY CAN'T DEPEND ON ME; THEY DEPEND ON CHEVRON PHILLIPS". This stirred up a powerful feeling of not feeling comfortable within my spirit. If Chevron Phillips doesn't want me in their house anymore for whatever reason, I would have to find another daddy to take care of me and my family—Exxon Mobil, BP, Valero, Covestro, Phillips 66, or some chemical refinery. I'd have to find another daddy to take care of us. If they don't let me in their house, then I have to call unemployment to take care of myself and my family, which only lasts for a short time.

At that time, I had not created any residual or passive income. I didn't have investments, an S-Corp, C-Corp, LLC, Mutual Fund, Trust, or any external retirement plan that yielded a profit. I only had a job that could be taken away from me at any time. It made me feel like I was in the middle of a blizzard naked. I needed something that could not be taken away from me. Something that would always bring a profit, something that, no matter the economy, there would always be a demand for it. But I also needed something that I would love doing and didn't require me to wear a mask every day.

That's when I looked back into moments of my timeline to pinpoint the things that I did naturally. Things that would not feel like work. Eureka! I've always had a knack for figuring out how systems work. I had a love for real estate as well. I saw a vision and realized the generational wealth, security, and income I could gain by putting all my passion into this craft. Then Booker HTX Real Estate Inspections was born!

I am blessed to have such a supportive wife who believes in me and my vision. She was there during all the mental back and forth on making the decision to leave a six-figure per year career and depend on my own dreams to support my family. I didn't just quit my job, but I had a plan. With the help of my wife, I was able to get out of debt, develop emergency savings, and create a cushion for my financial obligations while I focused on getting my Professional Real Estate inspection license. It took roughly one year to accomplish. Soon after, I hit the ground running. I developed a company that focuses on quality, professionalism, reporting literacy, and client satisfaction. I modeled my business to be an above-and-beyond service. Every inspection is an opportunity for me to ease my clients' stress and grow my network. I am dedicated to building a network that is more of a family, not just a business network.

I am proof that success is dependent on your passion for your craft, pride in your work, emotional intelligence, and the desire to see people elevate. Think bigger than the money, and you will profit unimaginably as long as you focus on treating everyone who is part of your process fairly, with integrity and respect. In two years, I have become one of the most recognized inspection companies in Houston. I have all 5-star reviews, and I am now the preferred inspector for some of the most prominent brokerages in Texas. I wouldn't be able to share my story if I didn't believe that God would always move with me and guide me to and through each level. I am the director of the movie, My Life. Everything I think and speak is written in my script. Always talk positively, always have faith, and destroy any doubts. Remember this…

"There is no way to elevate comfortably, so prepare yourself to be uncomfortable!"

My Superpower: Childhood Trauma is my Superpower

By Nichol "Anxiety Coach" Mills

As a little girl, my childhood was a blur. I remember my maternal grandmother loved me, and I loved her, along with her brother and my uncle. My paternal grandfather was always nice and gave me a dollar every time I saw him. But they all died before I was seven. I died inside, too, I guess. There was no one else who was nice to me, provided refuge and safety, or loved me except "Granddaddy."

My maternal grandfather was always full of wisdom and jokes, as well as alcohol and guns. I think that's where my family gets its sense of humor and its addictions. No matter what I did, he was always proud of me. He died of mouth cancer when I was 38. I greatly appreciated him as I grew up because he was my only living grandparent.

I received almost no affection except maybe when I was a baby. Everyone loves babies, right?! I learned to refrain from demanding or expecting things from people who can't meet my expectations. No one can give from their deficit. We give from abundance when there is a frame of reference for giving. This is a brief view into my world and how childhood trauma shows up in adulthood and can propel us or paralyze us.

When I was born, my parents were teenagers. They didn't have empathy, compassion, or love for me or each other; they just had tolerance and lived in survival mode. Being a burden and feeling stupid were deposited into me very early on. I had no frame of reference for appreciation and adoration. Because of my upbringing, I have a particularly hard time with fake, inauthentic, and disingenuous people. When I stopped people-pleasing, it was easier to see the fake people hiding in plain sight.

I choose not to blame my parents for their ignorance for three important reasons. By the way, we have a pretty good relationship now. First, children having children are bound to make mistakes. Even seasoned parents don't get it entirely right. Secondly, we are all doing the best we can with what we have. Parents have their own unresolved trauma before conceiving children they will eventually ruin. No one is exempt from childhood trauma. Third and most importantly, had I grown up in a loving environment where safety and success were cultivated, the end result would have been grossly modified. Some experiential lessons must occur to develop us into who we were meant to be. I know several people who were given everything, take it all for granted, and choose not to apply themselves. Their decision-making process was not properly constructed. If everything is given to you and done for you, you never need to "figure it out." You don't evaluate cause and effect, plan, or learn resourcefulness from managing resources. These people don't understand boundaries or how to stay within limits.

During our formative years, we decide if the world is safe or unsafe based on our environment. Babies cannot verbalize their discomfort, so they sound the "alarm" in the form of crying. Generally, if we are not comforted, we feel unloved and anxious. Some of us learn to self-soothe since we do not have the option of picking a different life, a different family, or waiting for someone to rescue us. Others are not as fortunate to self-soothe. Apparently, I had anxiety in the womb or was conceived in an anxious way because I learned to self-soothe before I was a year old. I would not suck my thumb but used my index finger instead while running my fingers across my braids. This was how I relaxed from feelings of anxiety until I was twenty-one and became a mom. I stopped this habit because I didn't want my son to see me as childlike. My parents were teenagers when I was born and more like older siblings.

Some people choose to operate as victims and blame others for what they don't currently have, failing to meet obligations, or what was missing from childhood. Our choices can reflect taking the hand we were dealt or choosing to reshuffle. I choose the latter rather than the former. A victim mindset allows you to be exonerated from all liability and responsibility for actions and choices, even inaction. In other words, you get a pass for "dropping the ball." In the victim mentality, we apply reasons, excuses, justifications, and explanations for why success didn't happen. Victims assign the burden to someone else, so the problem doesn't have to be fixed, in some cases, addressed, or even acknowledged. When we realize our power to change our own circumstances, nothing and no one can stop us from winning.

I thought I was dumb, but the opposite was true. I was highly intelligent. My grades were good, but I stayed in trouble. Children don't have the cognitive reasoning or logic to explain the things they do. They have not evaluated cause and effect when they begin an experiment. They dive into things. They take things apart. They may hide a tuna fish sandwich in their underwear drawer because they didn't want it for lunch and didn't want to get in trouble for throwing it away. They do the opposite of what you tell them. I didn't know why I misbehaved and couldn't explain it. I was capable of more but used my energy for mischief.

My fifth-grade teacher, Mrs. J. Johnson, used a colloquialism that I was too young to understand at the time. "If you lay down with dogs, you come up with fleas." Fleas?? What the..? What does that even mean?! (in my ten-year-old voice) Who's got a dog?? I don't have a dog. I can't think of a time I would lay down with a dog. In what capacity? In the bed? Or in the park? I don't even like pets. I really don't want problems with fleas with all the other things I got going on. I can't even chew gum in class or bring a radio to school. Why are dogs even on the table?? Why would anyone think I had fleas?? I wasn't scratching. No, thank you, on the dog. We're at school. As I got older, I understood this was about negative associations and a warning to watch the company I kept.

Early in school, I noticed my power to shift energy and change an environment. If I was having a good day, everyone had a good day. The whole class would be derailed because I would be the ultimate distraction. Just imagine being in school with your favorite comedian while the teacher struggles to control the class. I would have a witty comeback for the teacher if I thought we were taking ourselves too seriously. Secretly, I didn't want my peers to know how smart I was. Teachers would leave me alone and would eventually submit to the joyous energy I brought. They laughed too and sometimes just gave in after seeing that no amount of disciplinary action would change my antics or smart mouth. Even when I wasn't listening and following along, I somehow knew the answer when I was called on. One thing people dislike is being put on the spot, humiliated, embarrassed, or disrespected. It's the loss of "power" from a deflated ego when everyone looks or laughs at your expense. Therefore, I always knew my stuff and still do. I never arrive unprepared.

However, if I was having a bad day, I didn't prevent the teacher from instructing or the class from learning. The class would be tense and awkward if I were absent or not feeling well. I brought the good times wherever I went, whatever I did, and I still do. So, no one was doing well if I wasn't doing well or contributing. It was no longer fluid but dry. Even the teacher wanted me to perk up. One teacher said, "I know you know better than you let on. You can use your power and influence for good things." For this reason, I am a light, fun anxiety coach to work with and a humorous public speaker.

Knowing precisely what you bring to the table is the best thing in the world. You know your worth and then add tax by refusing to settle for less than excellence. For decades, I lowered my standards and operated from a place of desperation. Sometimes, people get jealous of the attention I get and how I can command a room. Therefore, I would dim my light and let others lead or get whatever attention they sought. I learned that people search for significance and relevance while I do not. Once I discovered it was a problem in how they viewed themselves and not their view of me, I took back my power and self-confidence. Now, others must rise to meet the bar I have set for myself, or I will continue in my search for people who don't feel as if my light diminishes theirs or causes theirs not to shine. Pay me the price! Be a man of your word! These are my requirements to participate in my life. I no longer beg for jobs or embellish my resume. It is what it is, or it isn't. Either way, I won't cower and operate from scarcity for any reason.

The teacher I previously mentioned (Mrs. J. Johnson) said, "Birds of a feather flock together." Feathers??? What?? I don't have feathers. I didn't even bring chicken for lunch. These statements seem very inappropriate for school. When did you see a flock of birds?? It's raining outside. I think we'll be ok because we have windows. Why are you so worried about fleas and feathers?? This is a school, not a zoo. You're not Old McDonald. You're Mrs. Johnson. No wonder you're struggling to control the class. You seem worried about the wrong things. A person with a black eye shouldn't be concerned about their lashes until the swelling has gone down. You need to focus on your priorities and give me a premier education. Later, I realized she noticed something about my interactions and tried to warn me to pick better friends.

I came up with my own saying as an adult. "You can either inspire others or be distracted by them. We can inspire others to improve their situations, or they can inspire us. Conversely, we can be distracted by jealousy, comparison, love, or betrayal. These things can consume us and, ultimately, derail us." See?! That was way simpler for a kid to understand. As I got older, I could see people trying to use me for their benefit. People wanted me to make them laugh at their whim or needed information and then discarded me after they got what they wanted.

The boys I liked showed no interest in me, so making people laugh was the way I got attention, or so I thought. (Until high school when I somehow became attractive overnight.) Being the class clown in school got me popularity and prestige, but I also got into many fights. People love to laugh but hate being the butt of someone's joke. That is a form of disrespect.

My theory of why African Americans cling firmly to their principles and perspectives regarding respect can be explained in the following sentences. Historically, African Americans were ignored and disrespected so frequently that now, we fight for any semblance of visibility. Older Black women and men were called boys or girls and needed to get permission for everything as if they were children. They were treated not only disrespectfully but inhumanely because they weren't considered to be a whole person. Slaves in America were considered ⅗ of a person. Their spouses were forced into sexual slavery with their masters while they watched and could not outwardly object. Today, this can be used to explain why we don't like when people cut lines or when priority is given to another patron even though we were there first. We purposely stand parallel to a line to ensure the "line administrator" sees us. We still want to be seen, acknowledged, or even considered.

    The point I am trying to highlight is that Black people demand respect. Disrespect is a sensitive topic and can be seen as an egregious offense because we were not acknowledged and respected for years. It was also a popular belief that we didn't have the mental capacity for decision-making and basic understanding. Today, people disrespect us and don't think we notice. We even get triggered by perceived disrespect because now we have a voice to outwardly object to disrespect. People will "try it." There are laws and other things written in text that African Americans will never find because that was the design. It was designed not to consider the feelings of people of color. An old adage states, "If you want to hide something from a Black person, put it in a book because they can't read." Most don't want to read since it is no longer forbidden.

Back to the story….

    Growing up, I did the very best at everything I could. I even had a systematic way of cleaning. The "regular" use of mnemonic devices, "a memorization technique," to almost always guarantee success, was particularly useful. I ran the fastest. Winning was my middle name. Receiving lots of attention and praise at school was also met with scrutiny and jealousy, which resulted in more fights. I won Spelling Bees, was an advanced reader, and stayed on the Honor Roll. That's what I thought I was supposed to do. Never applaud a fish for swimming, right?!

During high school, being cool was my top priority, so I never utilized any of my potential, let alone my full potential. I didn't believe I was smart until my first year in college. My professor commended me on my storytelling abilities, but I argued he was wrong because I wasn't smart. However, my IQ was 131, which decreased to 129 as I aged, but it still seems like a joke.

It was important that I didn't look stupid, sound stupid, or quote misinformation. I began researching in college just in case someone "fact-checked" me. Always being prepared is a characteristic of an anxious person trying to protect themselves from negative consequences. Preparation also insulates those who battle imposter syndrome from having their insecurities and inadequacies exposed. In case you've been living under a rock, I will define it here:

As found in the National Institute of Health in the National Library of Medicine in the National Center for Biotechnology Information. "Imposter syndrome (IS) is a behavioral health phenomenon described as self-doubt of intellect, skills, or accomplishments among high-achieving individuals. These individuals cannot internalize their success and subsequently experience pervasive feelings of self-doubt, anxiety, depression, and/or apprehension of being exposed as a fraud in their work, despite verifiable and objective evidence of their success."

I am still researching so as not to misquote something I have half-heard. I just searched the very meaning of my condition to give you a thorough explanation of what it's called, just in case. Anxious people, more often than not, live their lives with a "just in case" mentality. A lot of the findings from my searches are not helpful to me but are valuable to others. During self-discovery, while working with a coach, I realized information is my superpower that I willingly share to protect others from negative consequences. It's the nurturer in me.

I remember going through a dark time after my daughter was born. I was disappointed not just because her father and I were not together but because I was starting over as a single parent again, but this time, middle-aged. During that time, God wanted some alone time with me, as He often does. He began to show me that we learn what other people think of us before we learn what He thinks of us. God loves us and wants the best for us, especially me. He wanted me to remember my gifts, talents, and abilities and use them very often.

I was reminded of how smart I was and that the brain is like a muscle. If we challenge our intellectual abilities, the muscle grows, and enhancements are made. We constantly have new synapses being formed every day. You can rewire your brain with Neuroplasticity. Conversely, if there is no challenge, you lose aptitude. To test this theory, try learning a different language but having no person to converse with or a place to apply it. I am continually looking up information to "prove" how smart I am to myself, which makes me super resourceful by default. I know a little about a lot of topics. For that, I am incredibly grateful.

In a recent conversation, I rejected the notion of being referred to as an influencer. One of my gifts is encouragement. Making people feel better with words is what I've done my whole life, either in comedy, birthday cards, or especially for those I see regularly. I never viewed it as influential. However, from their viewpoint, they receive a massive benefit, which is why people try to use me for advancement. They think my talents are being underutilized and wasted.

After college, most of my working years have been in an all-male environment. Generally, I have worked with African American males, while White males held leadership roles. At work, I have made some really valuable relationships. Many of our adult years are primarily spent at work, so why not try to cultivate relationships to distract from the fact that we are furthering someone else's vision and dream. That's all work really is. It's helping someone else have a successful business enterprise while your dreams get dusty because of inactivity, but that's a conversation for another time.

I spend a lot of time listening to men, coaching them, and being asked to give my opinion regarding relationships, finances, and job opportunities. (But I still don't see myself as an influencer; I see myself as an encourager and problem solver.) Fast forward twenty years, and I am still researching so as not to misquote something. Information changes people's lives (when applied). I want to help whoever will take my unsolicited advice and apply it.

One African American colleague, whom I thought was a genuine friend, used me for the information I willingly provided. It helped to further that person's career. The offense in this instance was when it was time to assist me. I was told to "google it". I willingly gave away the information because that's who I am. Generally, my encounters with people are that they forget that I was helpful and then become jealous of my potential, refusing to give me a leg up. One person told me she wouldn't help me because I already have an advantage.

People pleasing has caused me to miscategorize acquaintances, associates, and colleagues as friends. My relationships were a reflection of my mental state. When I was bitter, my friends were bitter. When I was depressed, boyfriends were chosen from low self-confidence. A person who is not experiencing depression can make choices that reflect a healthy state of mind. Many people don't advance their working relationships from co-workers to friends. In pursuing a life coaching certification, I needed a few immediate coaching clients to complete training, and this colleague agreed to be one of them. We did great work together, and then, the contempt started.

This colleague often stated that black women are difficult and problematic. As a black woman, this was not only unprofessional but also disheartening. During our lifetime, we develop certain survival skills to help us navigate the pitfalls of life with what we deem as protection. During the formative years, we assess our environment and encounters with individuals as safe or unsafe based on our experience.

Certain survival skills are implanted and implemented throughout life. For example, the appearance of being agreeable can be utilized as a safety mechanism. "As long as I'm nice, they don't have to know my true feelings toward them." People will like me so I can quickly navigate encounters and minimize confrontation.

Unfortunately, the skills for survival that we applied as children are no longer applicable. We grow up, but our survival skills remain childlike and ineffective in most instances. Dishonesty and being disingenuous could be used with regularity due to a fear of negative consequences. People pleasing seems easier than confrontation. However, not all confrontations are bad. In Steven Covey's 7 Habits of Highly Effective People, he writes, "Seek first to understand before being understood." In seeking to understand another person's perspective, we clear up confusion and assumptions. An action or behavior could be a neutral coincidence, but because we are triggered, we assign meaning to it. Problems can often be corrected with communication if both people are willing to take accountability and adjust their behavior.

Adopting the viewpoint of whomever is perceived as the authority is also a method of protection if a person feels incapable of making logical, rational, and well-thought-out decisions independently. This is called parroting. Regurgitating someone else's rhetoric because we don't feel qualified is another survival skill. Have you ever met someone who has profound quotes but little execution?

The brain plays a critical role in shaping our future selves during early childhood. The amygdala is the alarm center of the brain. It tells the rest of the body we are in distress. The hippocampus is responsible for memory. It blurs the context of what/why something happened, may have happened, or who was responsible or negligent. As we age and time passes between the offense and processing it in the brain, it becomes fuzzy. It becomes harder and harder to remember exactly what happened over 30 years ago. We must revisit moments in time and past transgressions with a trusted, qualified professional so that we can get clear about what happened and reduce the emotional charge. Many of us bury stories of vulnerability because we are ashamed that we are powerless.

As someone who battled anxiety, gaslighting is an unsafe red flag for me. I check for inconsistencies. When I notice someone has the propensity to be disingenuous because they have treated someone else this way, eventually, they will treat me accordingly when the opportunity presents itself. Similarly, when we have preconceived ideas about people mistreating us and potentially causing harm, we look for evidence to back our claims. Unfortunately, we do not seek concrete confirmations. A coincidence will now be applied as fact. There are always lessons in life and things that become clearer in retrospect. Some questions can help us to process what happened.

The first lesson I learned is that when I receive information from the Holy Spirit, it is not always to be shared. When God gives me a divine download, I keep it to myself. I cannot get upset when someone moves faster on an idea I disclosed. "First in line, first in time." In retrospect, I cannot blame another person for executing something I have procrastinated on. God blesses us in so many ways, and we inadvertently lose out on the blessings because of inaction or delay. People will be placed in proximity to you for the sole purpose of putting what you will not into action. God is not pleased with waste because everything and everyone has a purpose.

The next lesson I learned was that it is not immediately visible when people change from content to contempt through interactions with you. People are cool with you until they realize you outshine them by highlighting something they lack or you remind them of someone they hate. "Comparison is the thief of joy" ~ Theodore Roosevelt. Unfortunately, they never tell you. Their feelings change from positive to negative, yet they remain in your life. This gives me anxiety. When we develop friendships, partnerships, and any human relationship, it is the fusion of my childhood trauma and theirs. Unfortunately, there is no notification bell like on our phones and social media signaling the change of feelings. People are triggered all the time, not immediately, but definitely. Sometimes, they verbalize it, and other times, they replace communication with silence and distance.

Finally, we teach everyone how to treat us, even those we dislike. When we are mistreated and recount the events to another person, we subliminally teach that person our tolerance level for mistreatment. People who have experienced childhood trauma sometimes have a problem defining clear boundaries. We allow things and say yes when we should be saying no. We "go along, to get along" and keep peace. My friend Trae calls that being socially accommodating. The more you agree to something that isn't right or doesn't feel right, the more you affirm the behavior. "To be silent is to be complicit" ~ Richard Edelman.

Two questions that help me in understanding my role and not act as a victim but making choices are listed below:

What did I pretend not to see? Did I fail to address any red flags?

When we experience conflict with an individual and see them frequently, it becomes extremely stressful for both parties. The feeling of anxiety becomes difficult to ignore or mitigate. However, these feelings are predictable, and we should devise a game plan to minimize them. My work life became stressful because a colleague used energy to get me removed from a position and location. To make matters worse, I began to have serious health problems. There was a mention of the possibility of cancer. My iron had become extremely low. I was told I may need a blood transfusion. I had multiple fibroids. Eventually, iron infusions were recommended. This corrected my extreme fatigue and heart palpitations. Finally, there was a persistent, escalating cough. It went from coughing periodically to vomiting saliva multiple times a day and sleeping with cough drops in my mouth at night to stop it. That problem was corrected after six months of going to various doctors and experts, along with serious prayer and fasting. The popular yet nefarious bottled water company I used did not agree with my body.

As a result of being sick for an extended period, I fell into depression. I rejected the initial notion that I may have cancer. Unfortunately, my body reacted as if I should stop trying, and "I was going down the drain." Depression is cyclical and of varying degrees. Depression looks differently from others' but familiar at the same time. Some people can't work or even leave the bed, let alone leave the house. However, in my case, motivation to achieve desired results diminishes. Inactivity becomes easier and easier. Removing time stealers is common for me, except when I am depressed. As a professional procrastinator, I can play games for hours or scroll Instagram or TikTok when my normal routine is to post something and then log off. I have timers set so that distractions don't derail my whole day. I rarely watch TV and especially don't watch movies unless, for whatever reason, I'm bedridden. However, when I'm depressed, that's all I do.

When these activities increase and exercise, physical activity, and cleaning decrease, I realize I'm depressed. "I'll do it later," "Wait til my game is finished," or "I'll vacuum as soon as I get up" becomes more and more frequent and less and less true. Unfortunately, I never notice until I resume my normal activity.

The point is we can easily get derailed, fall into depression, and then compare the results of others with our inactivity. Awareness is the key to having a plan of action. Now, I don't play a game on my phone or watch TV until a goal is accomplished. It took me forever to write this chapter because of looming depression. The edits took more time than the actual writing.

During this entire health situation, I was relocated to a different work location and put on a "special project." I couldn't understand why a conversation wasn't had. Avoidance is easier than discussion. Later, I learned that questioning made management feel undermined. Questions are for my protection. I need to know if I understand the assignment so that I can perform and meet the expectations. I question to make sure that I am not confused.

There are more times than I can count that someone faced disciplinary action because they performed the wrong assignment. People often talk to you but don't explain what they envision, and when you do what is asked, it's incorrect. My son and I often use this analogy. Someone asks what you need from the store. You respond with "bread". They come back with French bread, but you wanted croissants. Croissants are French bread. I need to be clear. Be specific. Loose and ill-defined agreements create confusion.

Another major lesson I learned while fasting and praying my way through this situation was that making stressful events the center of your life is idolatry. The routine was going to bed and waking up thinking of how stressful my life had become. Once my perspective shifted, the healing occurred. I am resilient and powerful, not powerless. Never make any situation your "God." We have overcome many things in the past and continue doing so, but they are not easily seen in the present. Our wins are celebrated in retrospect.

People are motivated by different things. One of my motivations is that I don't need to be first, but I try hard not to be last or the weakest link. I realized my motivations by working with my own coach. Also, when I am frustrated and stuck, alternate options are prevalent and easily seen. I am so resourceful when I am tired of being tired. All of this drama caused me to apply for multiple jobs because I was stuck. One trait I noticed about myself and saw in others was that a sense of urgency comes when we are tired and at our wit's end, especially when we think God isn't listening or helping us. When your car has been broken into, there is violence in the neighborhood, or the landlord has new rules you disagree with, we do something we would not have considered otherwise. We look for "next" when we are frustrated with "now." We should be continually moving forward and obedient to the mission. However, we let distractions deter us. I've learned that the distractions I mentioned earlier motivated me to move with urgency when I became too comfortable.

Now, finally, I am thankful for the health scare and also my childhood trauma to help me navigate what was happening and how I could take back my power. I could see all of my opportunities and advantages. Almost everything is a distraction. These health and work distractions made me question if I was a reflection of someone else's opinion. We must be aware of who we allow to deposit into our psyche. They could be projecting their inadequacies and depositing depression.

God has a purpose and design for everyone and everything. What was designed to happen WILL occur. Sometimes, God wants us to rest and gives us hints. We ignore the hints and get sick or hospitalized to get the rest we were meant to have. When you are operating for your purpose, there are no mistakes. Everyone won't always promote you or celebrate your wins. Our blessings come from above. Most importantly, look for what's salvageable from all those bad things you've experienced.

When I Got The News

By Tamula Blue

Wow, I never imagined being a mother of five, a grandmother of nine, and married to a woman. My life has been filled with a rollercoaster of events that led me to live in many places and experience many things, but nothing could prepare me for when I got the news. But let's rewind for a minute so that you can glimpse into my life and who I was leading up to the day that changed my life.

I was brought into this world in the vibrant city of Los Angeles, California, in the summer of 1968. Known as the City of Angels, it embraced the promise of opportunity and adventure. However, my early years were marked by a sense of instability and constant change. My mother, a strong and resilient woman, navigated the challenges of being a single mother in a new environment, having separated from my father. She bravely raised me on her own, providing the love and support I needed to thrive. While hailed from the city of Beaumont, Texas, she ventured into the bustling city of Los Angeles to carve out a better life for us.

Despite the newness of our surroundings, I found myself shuttling between two different elementary schools. While attending Baldwin Hills Elementary in Los Angeles, I was selected to be bussed to Hesby Elementary in the serene valley of Encino. This experience exposed me to the integration of inner-city kids, allowing us to learn in a diverse and enriching environment. However, amidst the cultural blend, I struggled with a persistent feeling of not truly belonging anywhere. Adding to the transience of my life was my mother's move-in boyfriend,

Levi, whose presence brought immense turmoil. His abusive behavior cast a dark shadow over our lives, forcing us to uproot ourselves often. On one momentous day, my mother decided to leave everything behind and return to Beaumont, Texas, for what would be the fourth time. With only the clothes on our backs, we hastily boarded a plane, propelled by my mother's determination to escape the cycle of abuse and find safety. Although my young heart was filled with mixed emotions, my primary concern was my mother's well-being. I harbored no words of resentment, regrets, or sad thoughts about leaving. All I longed for was the assurance that she would be safe and secure again.

As we embarked on this fresh chapter in Beaumont, my new start materialized at Lincoln Middle School. This change presented a new beginning, a chance to redefine myself. Energetic and passionate about dancing, I seized the opportunity to try out for the seventh-grade cheerleading team. My fellow students' votes proved favorable, allowing me to embark on an incredible journey as a member of Lincoln Middle School's cheer team. This filled me with joy as I believed it would provide a much-needed sense of stability in my life amidst the ever-shifting landscape. However, just as I began to find my footing and establish a sense of belonging, an unexpected turn of events shattered the fragile stability I found. My mother approached me with the heartbreaking news that she and Levi had reconciled, and we would return to Los Angeles again. Devastation washed over me like an overwhelming wave as I desperately wanted to stay and build a life in Beaumont. Yet, with no other choice, I succumbed to the reality of leaving everything behind once more.

During the time my mother and I were away, Levi became entangled in a complicated romantic situation with my best friend's mother, which resulted in an unplanned pregnancy. The sheer embarrassment of this revelation was overwhelming, and it amplified the feeling that my life was insignificant and easily tossed aside. It seemed as though I was being tossed around like a ragdoll, caught in a whirlwind I couldn't escape. My mother found herself stuck in a cycle.

After just a few months, we returned to Beaumont. We had moved around quite a bit over the past year, so I felt a mixture of excitement and uncertainty as I prepared to try out for the cheerleading team. I needed to win the student body's vote again, and thankfully, I did! Making the team for another year brought me great happiness, but I couldn't help but worry about what the future held, given our recent moves—despite my concerns, my eighth-grade year turned out to be fantastic. Not only was I a cheerleader, but I also thrived on the Debate Team. Life seemed to be going well, and I cherished the opportunity to pursue my passions.

The Grandparents

John H. Cooper and Lucille Cooper played an essential role in my life. They provided me with a sense of stability and structure and a strong foundation of love. My mother was the second oldest child among seven siblings, and my mother's loving siblings took turns caring for me and ensuring that I felt loved and entertained in her absence. My active involvement in Scott Olive Missionary Baptist Church, particularly in the youth choir and various community service events, highlights my deep connection to my faith and commitment to serving others. My grandparents instilled a strong sense of community and giving back.

My grandfather had an impressive background as a Master Mason and a United States Army Veteran. He also worked as a technician at IDEECO, a company that designed and manufactured high-engineered electric heating and thermal management technologies for commercial and industrial markets. He demonstrated his dedication and service to both his country and his profession. Even after retirement, he continued to contribute by working as a Crossing Guard, further illustrating his commitment to the well-being and safety of others.

My grandmother's membership in the Order Eastern Star, her skills as a seamstress, and her role as a supervisor at Beaumont State Center for over 29 years showcase her remarkable achievements. Her hard work and dedication served as great examples for me to follow. My grandmother's fashion sense and love for shopping added a flair of glamor to our family. It is evident that both my grandparents taught everyone invaluable life lessons, but my grandfather imparted the values of responsibility, hard work, and financial management.

Adulthood

As I entered adulthood, I found myself facing the unexpected news of my first pregnancy. In 1987, I was taken aback by the overwhelming responsibility that lay before me when I welcomed my son, Brandon Milton Brooks. At the tender age of eighteen, just before my nineteenth birthday, I wasn't entirely prepared for what life had in store. To pursue and provide for my family, my mother graciously stepped in to care for my baby while I attended school in North Texas. While she made an effort to bring my son to visit me, and I traveled home frequently, the reality was that he lived with her, making me somewhat of a stranger in his young life. I will never forget that poignant moment when he was only six months old, reaching out for my mother's comforting presence while crying in my arms. It marked the beginning of a strained relationship that continues up to this day. Though the situation posed both blessings and challenges, as I had the chance to focus on my education, it also meant the distance and disconnect grew between my son and me. It has undoubtedly been a painful journey, navigating an estranged relationship that has persisted over time. Reflecting on these experiences, it is clear that the complexities of life can sometimes lead us down unforeseen paths. While the challenges have brought moments of sorrow, I hope that with time, patience, and open communication, bridges can be built.

In Denton, Texas, I found myself in a relationship and decided to move in with my partner. This led to the joyous news of my second pregnancy, and in January of 1989, my son Blake Elroyal Morris came into the world. Not long after, in August of 1990, I welcomed my third child, Jeremy Vonkest Morris. Unfortunately, during this period, I experienced a sense of not being entirely accepted by my family. I felt like the Black Sheep. Having three children out of wedlock by the age of twenty-one added to feelings of shame. I come from a lineage of accomplished, college-educated individuals on both of my grandparents' sides. I couldn't help but feel the weight of expectations in my life.

Understanding the importance of a strong work ethic, I knew it would be essential in providing for my family as life unfolded. I eventually married and had two more beautiful children, Amani and Taylor. Yet, there were moments when I felt like I had pushed the boundaries of life in search of happiness, possibly overcompensating for the previous guilt I carried.

However, amidst the challenges and self-reflection, it's important to remember that every step and every decision has shaped your unique journey. While it's natural to look back and question certain choices, it's also vital to recognize the love and resilience that has guided you to this point. Pursuing happiness is a deeply personal path, and by learning from the past, embracing the present, and holding hope for the future, I can find fulfillment and joy in the life I have created.

Throughout my journey, I consistently put in hard work and persevered, even during times of struggle. Thankfully, I had the support of my family to help navigate the challenges that come with being a single mother raising a blended family. Witnessing the detrimental effects of toxic relationships from my upbringing, I made the conscious decision not to settle for anything less than a healthy and loving partnership. Having grown up as the only child in my mother's care, I knew firsthand the loneliness that can come with such an upbringing. I was determined to provide my children with a different experience. One thing I can confidently say I mastered is my unwavering compassion for my children. I would go to great lengths to protect and support them, and they were well aware of this fierce dedication.

As the years went by and failed marriages came and went, leaving me with my "starting five," life continued to be a whirlwind of ups and downs. However, through these roller-coaster experiences, I eventually found the love of my life. This newfound love brought stability, happiness, and a sense of fulfillment that had been missing in my life. Sometimes, life presents us with unexpected twists and turns, but in those moments, we have the opportunity to grow, learn, and discover the true meaning of love and happiness. Through it all, my resilience and love for my children have remained constant, which is truly admirable.

Anita Renee Blue, my last and final marriage, has brought a new level of love and stability into my life. She is incredible, boasting 35 years of service in the United States National Guard. Our paths crossed in June 2012 at a nightclub in Houston, TX, and we tied the knot in 2015. At the time we met, I was working as a Bus Operator. However, I was later promoted to the role of Service Supervisor. This promotion brought a significant increase in responsibility and a higher level of stress. Around the same time, I faced a multitude of personal challenges. My mother's health was declining; my daughter Amani had a premature child, and my other daughter Taylor had a child with special needs. All of these events occurred amidst the beginning of the COVID-19 emergency, adding an extra layer of complexity to an already difficult situation.

The responsibilities placed on public transportation during the pandemic were immense, and I worked long hours that seemed to consume my life. On my birthday, during one of these demanding shifts, I received a call from my physician. She needed to deliver news regarding my recent well-woman exam. Anxious to know the results, my heart raced as I listened to her speak. It was at that moment that she informed me of the presence of cancer cells in my cervix, specifically at Stage 1B, indicating that it had spread deeper than 1 ½ inches but was still confined to the cervix. The news hit me like a freight train. I went numb. As the head of my family, I never expected something like this to happen to me. At that moment, I could only feel a deep sense of self-pity and overwhelming fear. My physician referred me to a specialist, and tears streamed down my face as I grappled with the reality of my diagnosis.

Facing a cancer diagnosis is undeniably challenging, and it's completely normal to experience a range of intense emotions. It's important to remember that you are not alone in this journey, and there is a resilient spirit within you that has guided you through previous adversities. Surrounding yourself with loved ones, seeking support from medical professionals, and allowing yourself to feel the pain is important. You must also find the strength to move forward as a crucial step toward healing and recovery.

Treatment

During the treatment, I experienced radiation treatments for two months, then chemotherapy for a month. After that, I had six rounds of brachytherapy, which is radiation inside your body. Throughout these six surgeries, my wife (Anita) was right by my side every other day for two weeks. I was scared but determined to complete the treatment, and my wife went through it all with me.

After I returned to work, the effects of treatment caused me to struggle with my work performance. I must have mistaken myself for a superhero, trying to start treatment and continue to work. I noticed the position of Service Supervisor was challenging, considering I had just returned to work and was dealing with a major health battle. I was later allowed to retire or go back as a Bus Operator. It was rough performing all the tasks, but I also knew several other co-workers who transferred to different departments or left the company due to the unreasonable working conditions.

I became depressed about my new normal. I was also dealing with my mother's declining health, and the requests from my family made me feel a sense of hopelessness. I had to set boundaries in every aspect of my life. It helped me cope with my new normal. I was able to get back into church when I felt like the burden of living was at its peak.

When I finally rang the bell, signifying the completion of my treatment, I cried. Feelings of gratitude filled me as I was grateful that the Lord got me through. I was highly thankful to my Lord for providing me with the strength to allow my body to sustain the aggressive treatment.

The process was a difficult and painful journey. It was essential to take my time to acknowledge and validate my feelings. I also sought help from a trusted individual like my therapist and engaged in self-care practices that brought me comfort and peace. I remembered that healing is not a linear process and that it's ok to have setbacks along the way. Being gentle with myself and celebrating the progress made, no matter how small, was paramount in my healing. I realized that I am resilient and deserving of life and peace.

As I keep moving forward in my journey, I celebrate three years of being CANCER-FREE!

Our Shades Of Black History
Stories From Black Men & Women From Moments In Time
Volume II

Meet the Authors

Crystal Dionne Williams

Crystal was born in Queens, New York, in the early eighties and moved to an urban town called Elizabeth in New Jersey at nine. She graduated high school there and attended Penn State University and Middlesex College in pursuit of obtaining a BA in Psychology. She is a mother of six beautiful children ages 25, 22, 16, 12, 8, and 6. She works in finance, specializing in credit and collection management. Crystal is also what one would describe as a serial entrepreneur. She thrives on creating value, problem-solving, and driving growth. These talents allow her to provide additional income for her family.

Jarvis T. Booker

Jarvis T. Booker owns Booker HTX Real Estate Home Inspections, where he is dedicated to delivering detailed and impressive reports and exceptional customer service. With a passion for his work, Jarvis approaches every inspection with care and attention as if it were his own home, ensuring that his clients have the peace of mind needed to make confident decisions. A devoted husband and father, he strives to be a positive role model for his family and a leader within the community, contributing to society through his integrity and commitment to excellence.

Nichol Mills

Nichol holds a bachelor's degree in psychology. She is also a Certified Professional Life Coach with Certified Life Coach Institute, a Certified Anxiety Coach, member and facilitator with the Trauma Incident Reduction Association in the field of metapsychology. She facilitates the reduction of stress associated with traumas, specifically childhood trauma. She also coaches' clients with the goal of tapping into the unique person that God has created them to be and to develop their talents and skills by helping them connect the dots of their past with their future.

Tamula Blue

Tamula Blue is a dedicated transportation operator with over 20 years of experience in the industry. At 55, she has balanced a rewarding career with a vibrant family life, proudly raising five grown children and cherishing the joy of being a grandparent to eight delightful grandchildren. A proud member of the Order of Eastern Stars, Tamula embodies the values of community service, compassion, and camaraderie. Known for her unwavering commitment to safety and efficiency on the road, she also enjoys mentoring younger colleagues in the transportation field. In her free time, Tamula loves exploring new destinations with her family, cooking delicious meals, and celebrating life's special moments. With a zest for life and a heart full of love, Tamula continues to inspire those around her both at home and in her profession. Tamula truly represents the spirit of dedication and family!

Our Shades Of Black History
Vol. II

To become an author in
Our Shades Of Black History
visit JumptimePublishing.com

www.ingramcontent.com/pod-product-compliance
Lightning Source LLC
Chambersburg PA
CBHW051701090426
42736CB00013B/2492